**Requires Windows 95
or Mac 8.6 or higher**

Creative Clip Art for Classroom and Home
Created & Designed by Dianne J. Hook

ISBN:1-59441-312-6

Contents

Clip Art Assembly Basics 3

School Bear...4
School Bear Border..5
Terrific Mouse 6
Apples and Worms 7
Chalkboard Borders 8
Bear and Crayons...9
Giant Crayon Border.....................................10
Baxter Bear 11
Baxter Bear Border 12
Schoolhouses...13
Schoolhouse Border..14
Small Schoolhouse Borders 15
Schoolkids..16
Schoolkids Borders 17
Small Schoolkids Border 18
Bear Tags 19
Bear Tag Border 20
Small Bear Tag Borders 21
School Buses...22
School Bus Border 23
Backpacks and Boys 24
Boys and Books Border 25
Small Boys and Books Borders 26
Stars...27
Stars and Bear Border 28
Small Stars and Bear Borders 29
Award Ribbons..30
Ribbon Awards 31
Large Parchment Paper 32

Small Parchment Papers..................................33
School Tools..34
School Tools Border...35
Color Crayon Border.......................................36
Apples, Books, and Bears 37
Apples, Books, and Bear Border....................38
Small Apples, Books, and Bear Borders 39
Great Work Kids 40
Schoolhouse Kids Border 41
Teacher Bear Wood Border 42
Teacher Bear and Cubs Border 43
Small Teacher Bear and Cubs Border 44
Teacher Bear and Cubs Wood Border.............45
Small Cubs Wood Borders 46
School Tags 47
I Love My School 48
Small Waving Bear Borders 49
School Bear Desk Name Plates......................50
More Desk Name Plates..................................51
Bears and Hall Pass 52
A Note from Teacher.......................................53
Lined Notepad...54
Small Notepads 55
Tiny Notepads 56
Calendar with Header 57
Lined Awards/Bookmarks..............................58
Blank Awards/Bookmarks..............................59
Headers, Notes, Lists 60–61

Image Index 62-64

Credits

Illustrator: Dianne J. Hook
Content Design and Project Director: Sherrill B. Flora
Editor: Karen Seberg
Production: Mark Conrad
Cover Production: Annette Hollister-Papp

Clip Art Assembly Basics

Here are some suggestions as you make your flyers, announcements, or any project using clip art from this book.

Tools

Putting together the right tools will make your project go more smoothly and look better in the end. A good **copy machine** is a must. It's worth the extra effort to make sure your school or copy shop has machines that make clean copies. You will also need a bottle of white **paper correction fluid**, a fine-tip **black marker** to combine designs and add your own art to the project, **rubber cement** to mount the design onto your paper during the layout stage of your project, and **scissors** for cutting apart the designs you choose. Optional tools to help create a professional-looking project are a **nonreproducible blue pencil**, to make marks that will not show up on copies, a **proportion scale**, to help you determine the size of the reduction or enlargement necessary to fit your paper, and **blue grid paper** for laying out the project with straight lines.

Assembly Steps

1. Choose the design or designs you will be putting together for the project that you will be making.

2. Copy the design once from the book so that you have a copy from which to work without having to cut apart your book.

3. Cut out the designs from your copy and lay them out on your paper. (Blue grid paper comes in handy.) A light table can also help with the layout of your page.

4. Next, make a copy of the designs and any text on the paper before adding any other hand-drawn illustrations. Drawing over the grid paper lines is difficult and generally doesn't turn out well.

5. Now you have a good idea of what your project is going to look like. Go ahead and add all the extra finishing touches. Small doodles or even simple dots or squares can really "warm up" the page and keep it from looking choppy.

6. Make your final copies of the page. Easy!

Hints

- Keep a ¼-inch (0.64 cm) margin on all edges of your paper.
- If the edges of the cutout pieces are visible on your copies, lighten the copy machine one notch or use correction fluid on one copy and then use it to make the final copies.
- Removable tape is great for creating layouts if you will be using the design more than once.

Clip Art Images on CD

Clip art images presented in black and white in this book are available in both black and white and color on the enclosed CD. If desired, the images can be easily layered to create journal pages. The CD is Mac and PC compatible and requires an operating system of Windows 95/ Mac 8.6 or higher.

Have fun! You can become an artist and create wonderful projects for your class with the help of this book!

School Bear

My School is COOL

© Carson-Dellosa, illustrations © Dianne J. Hook DJ-604014

4

Terrific!

6

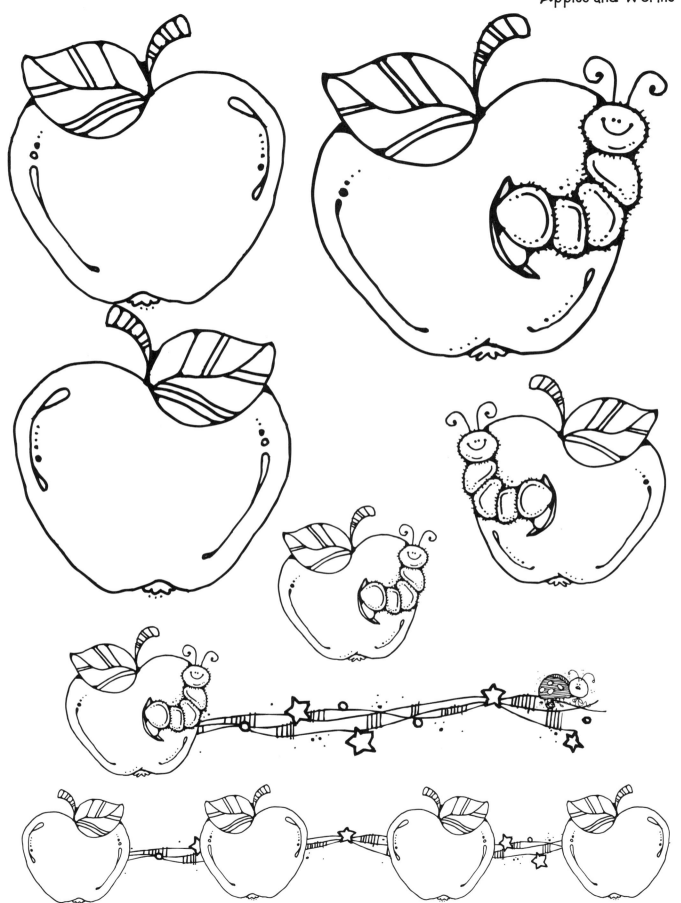

Schoolhouse Border

14

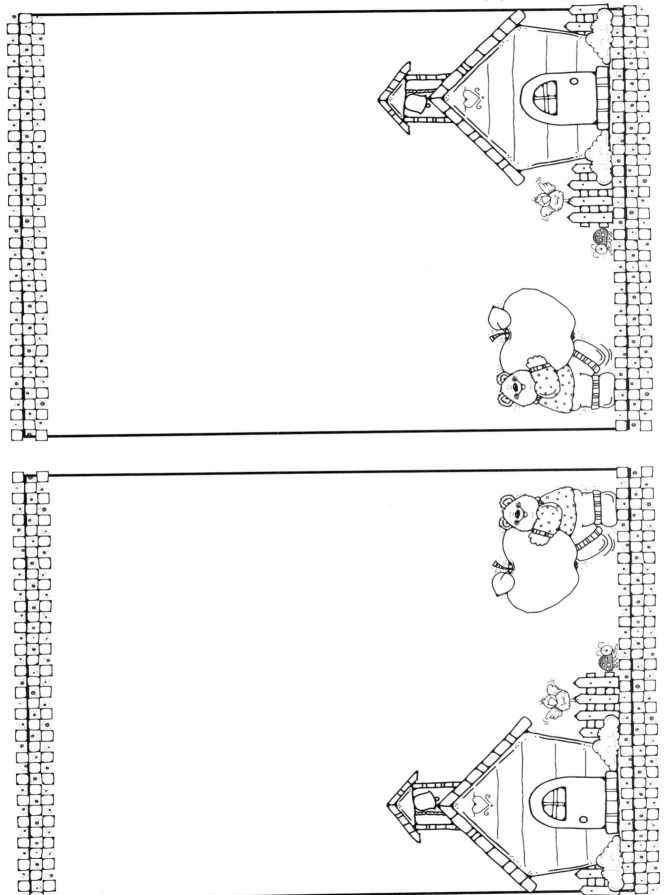

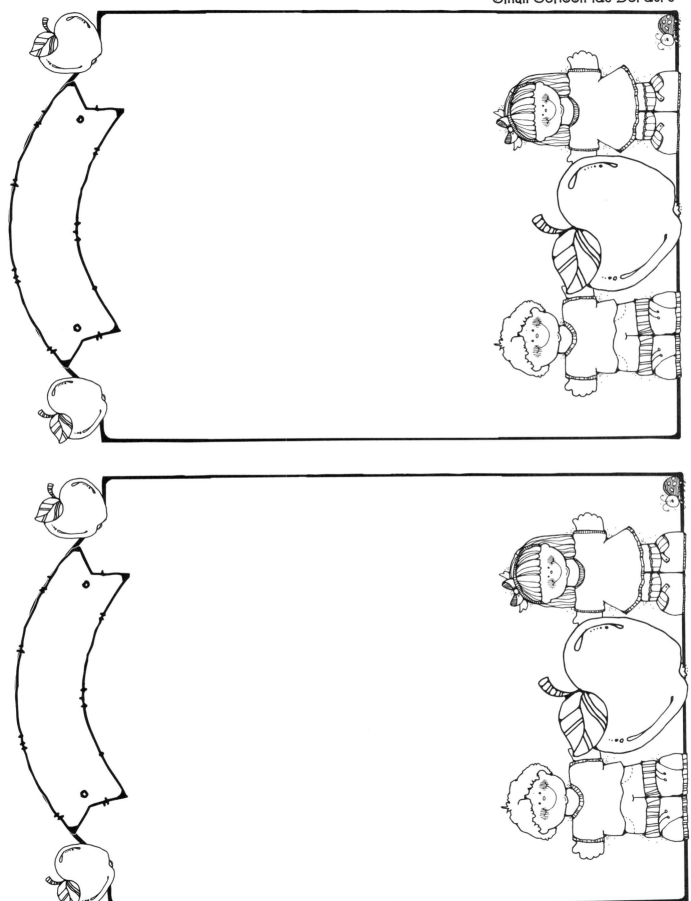

Bear Tags

Thank You!

Apple

19

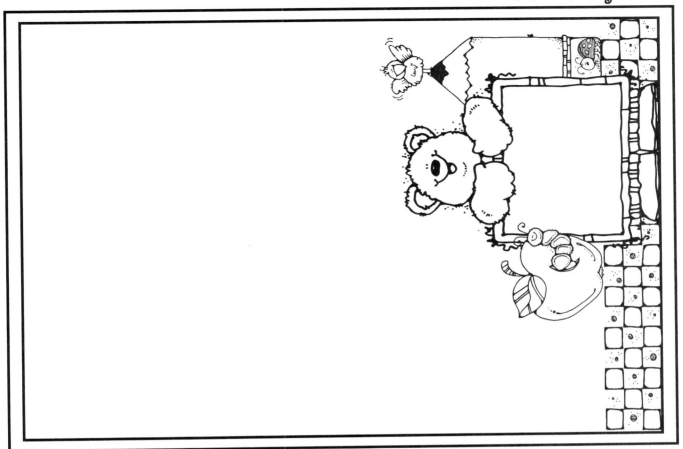

On our way...

Time for a Field Trip!

School Bus

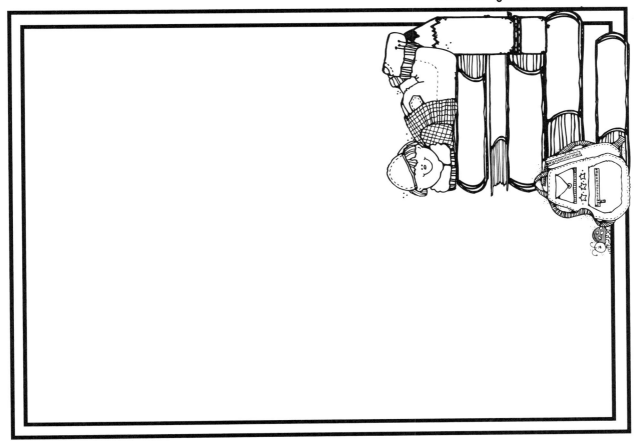

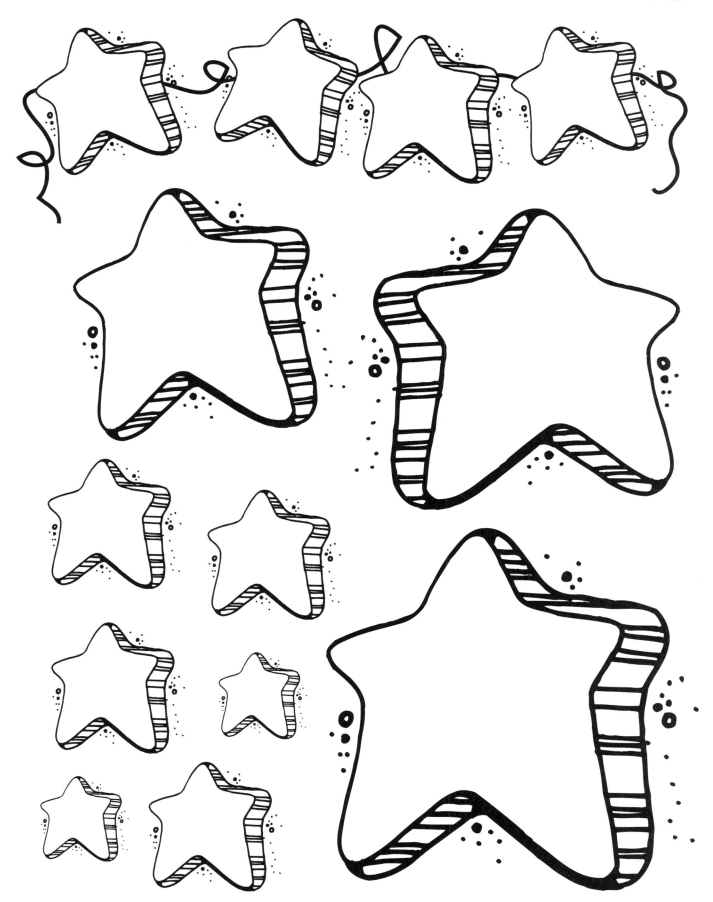

Hooray for YOU!!

_____

_____

_____

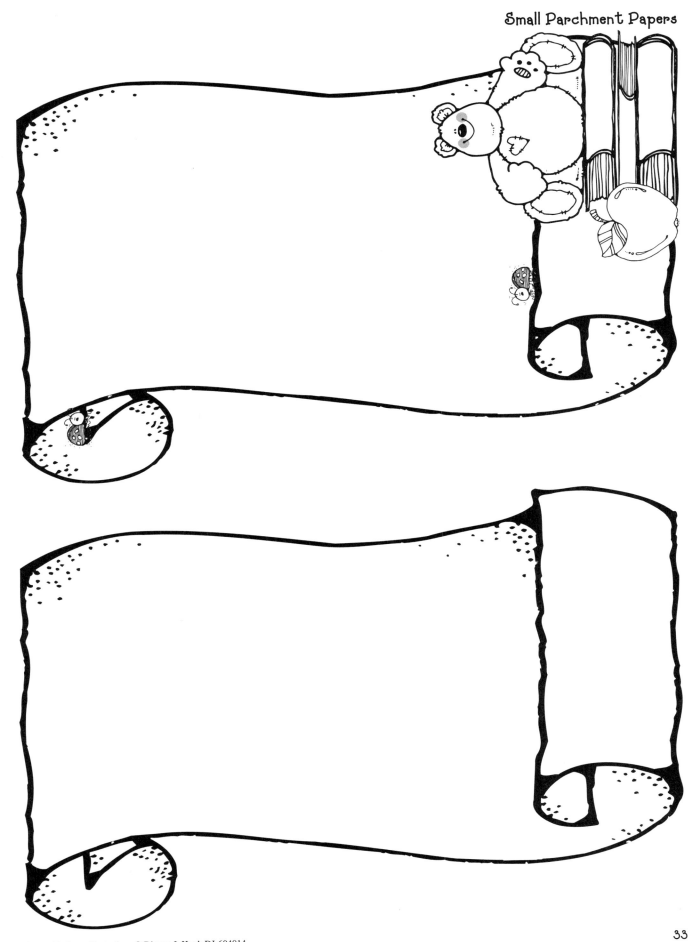

My Art Project

1 2 3 4 5 6
1 2 3 4 5 6 1 2 3 4 5 6 7

PASTE

1 2 3 4 5 6 7 1 2 3 4 5 6 7

Color Crayon Border

36

Apples, Books, and Bear Border

38

Back to School Night

School

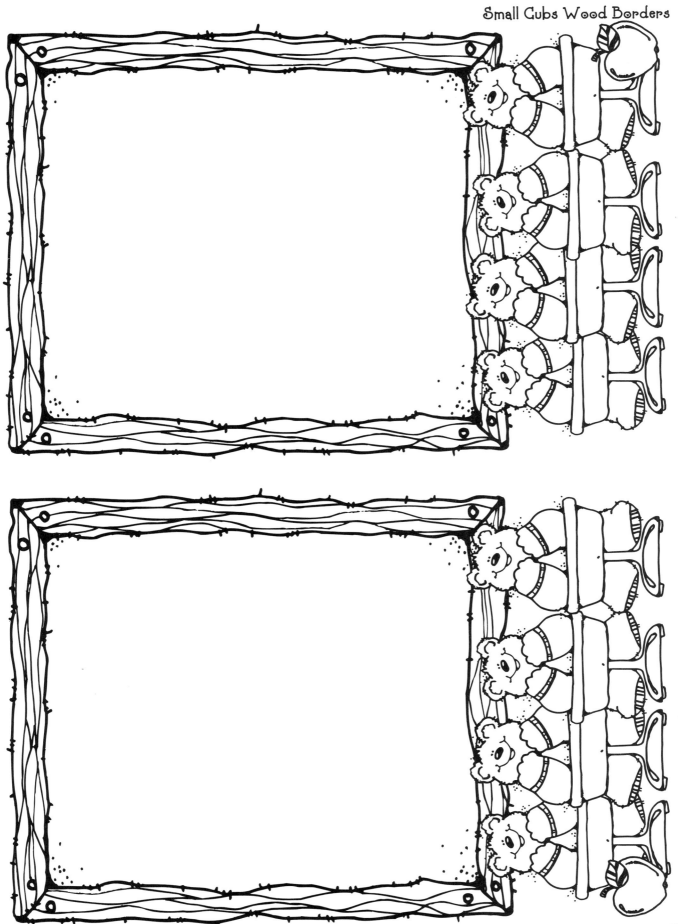

I
love my
school

Hall Pass

A Note from Teacher . . .

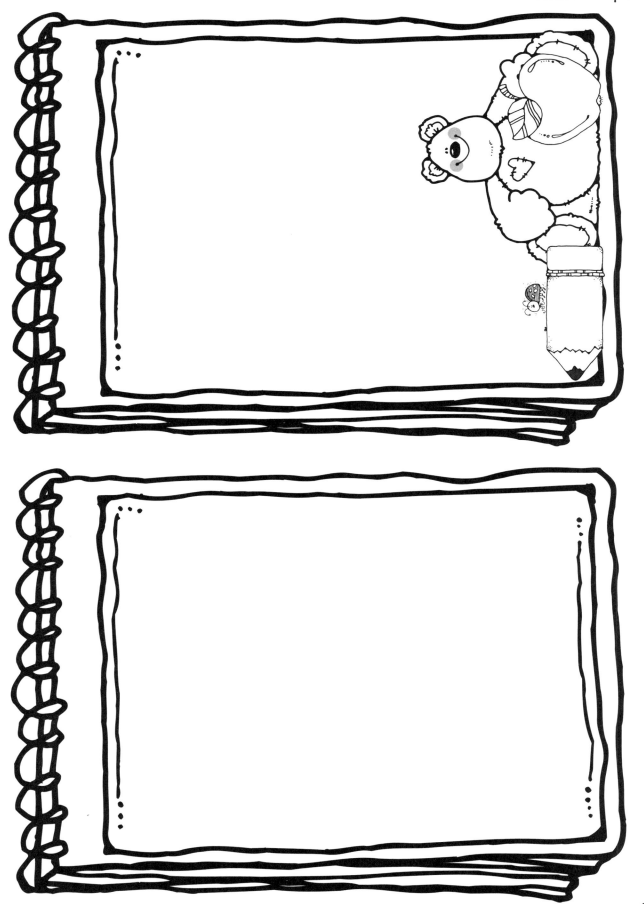

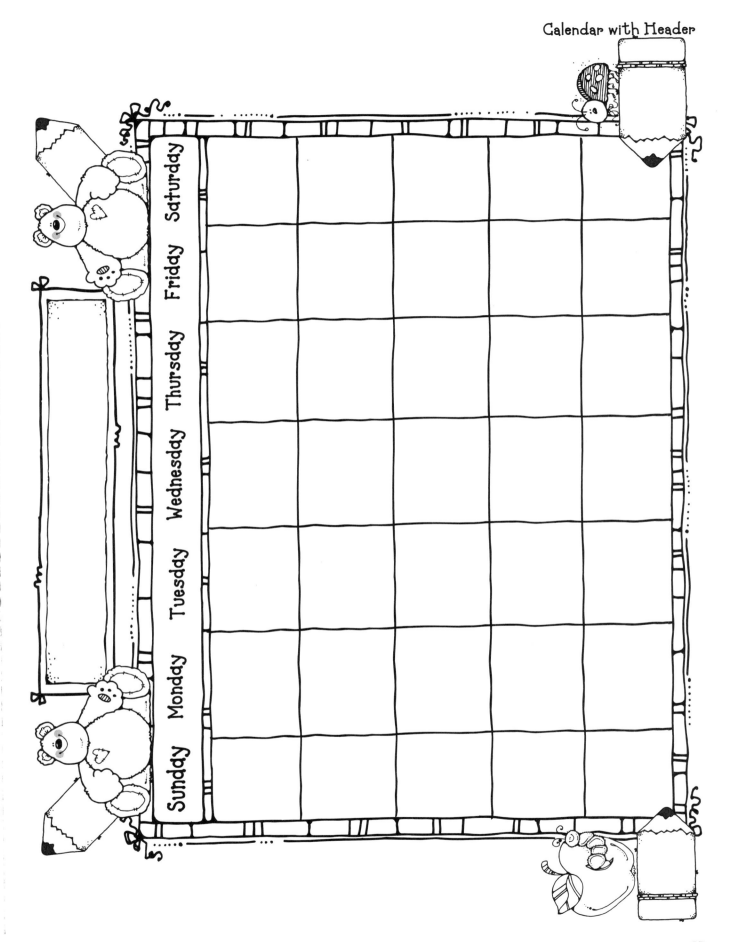

Sunday Monday Tuesday Wednesday Thursday Friday Saturday

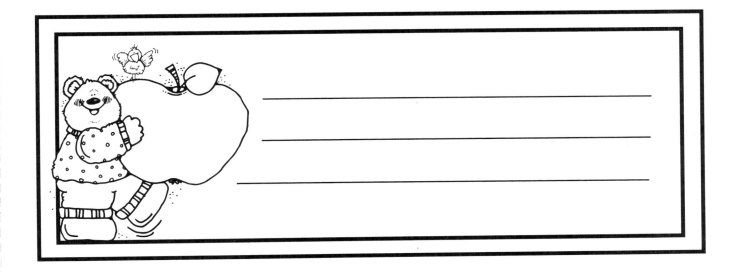

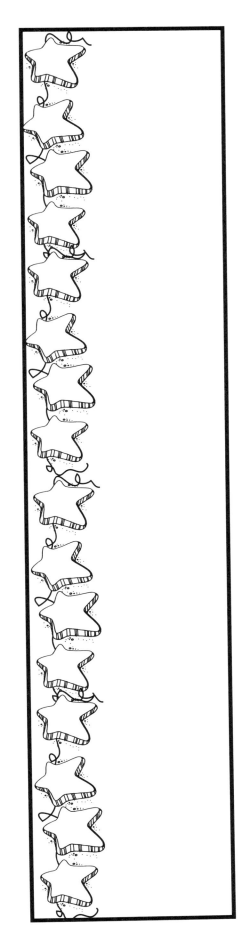

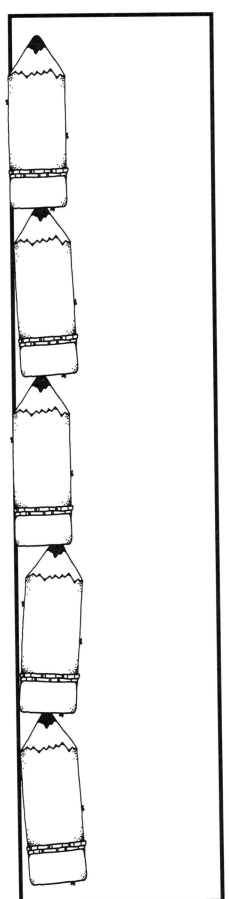

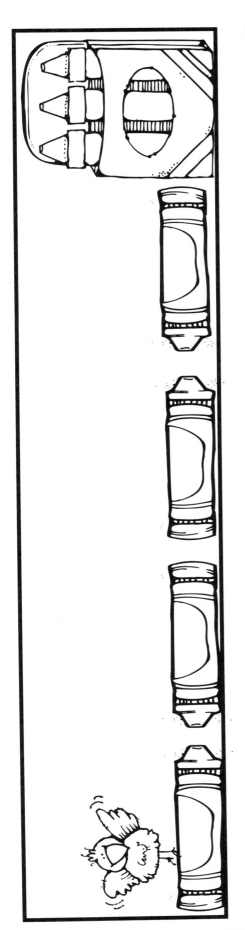

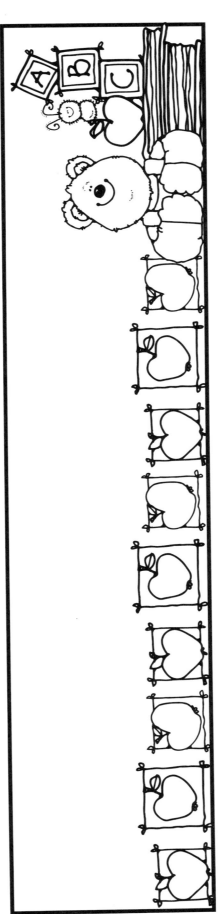

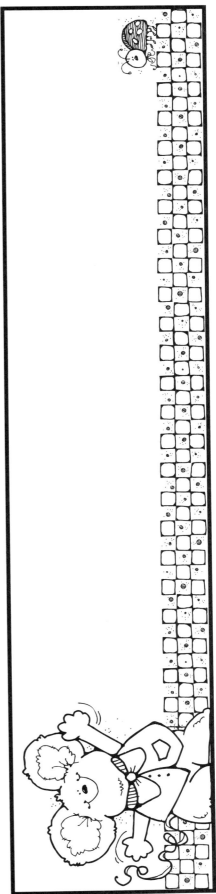

 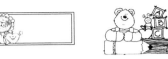

1staward   100award   abcbear   abcbooks   abcframe   abcnameplate

  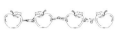

apple   applebear   applebearborder   appleborder   appleboxborder   appleboxframe

appleboxpage   appleframe   applemark   appleschool   applesign   applesquare   applesquareborder

appleworm   applewormborder   applewormframe   applewormpad   backpack   backpackmark

      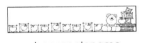

backtoschool   banner   bearapple   bearappleborder   bearappleframe   bearapplemark   bearapplename

 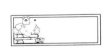

bearapplesign   bearbookmark   bearborder   bearcrayon   bearcrayonpage   beardeskframe   bearlean

    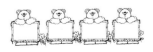

bearnameplate   bearscroll   bearscrollpage   bearsign   bearsignborder   bearstarframe   bearstarpage

bearthanks
 bearwave
 bearwavepage
 bigmouse
 birdie
 bookborder

books

 boybookstack

 boylay
 boywpen
 busborder
 busframe
 calendar
 classpage
 coolschool

 crayon
crayonborder
crayonname
 crayonsborder
 fantastic
 girlwapple
gradapple

Great Work!

greatwork
greatworklabel
hallpass
heartfeltbanner
 heartfeltbear
heartfeltbearbrdr
 heartfeltwpen

 kidappleborder
 kidsapple
 kidsapplepen
 kidsborder
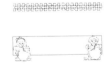 kidsnameplate
 kidswapple

ladybugborder
loveschool
loveschoolframe
mousemark
mousename
 mousewpen

 myartproject
 notepad
 notepadbear
 onourway
 openscissors
 paste
 pencil

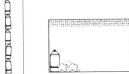

pencilframe   pencilmark   pennameplate   ribbon   road   ruler   rulerborder

rulers   schoolborder   schoolbus   schoolhouse   schoolhouseborder   schoolkidspage   schoolmark

schoolpad   scissors   scroll   squaredotsborder   star   starborder   starmark

Super!   **Terrific!**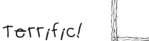

super   teacherframe   teachersframe   terrific   woodenframe   wormborder

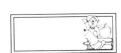   **WOW!**

wormmark   wormpad   wormsupplies   wormwave   wow   wowaward